Channel Islands National Park
and National Marine Sanctuary

Channel Islands National Park
AND NATIONAL MARINE SANCTUARY

Tim Hauf

TEXT BY CONGER BEASLEY JR.

Channel Islands National Park and National Marine Sanctuary

Photography: All photos © Tim Hauf, except where noted.
Text: Conger Beasley Jr.

Published by Tim Hauf Photography, P.O. Box 1241, Kingston, WA 98346, USA.

All rights reserved. No part of this publication may be reproduced,
stored in a retrieval system, or transmitted in any form or by any means,
electronic, mechanical, recorded, photocopied, graphic, or otherwise,
without the written permission of Tim Hauf Photography.

Copyright © 2008 Tim Hauf Photography

Library of Congress Control Number: 2007907462

ISBN: Hardcover – 978-0-9788219-2-0
        Soft cover – 978-0-9788219-3-7

Website: **www.timhaufphotography.com**
Email: timhauf@hotmail.com

Book design: Gretchen Scoble Design
Edited by: Cheryl Carnahan
Printed and bound in Korea

First printing: March 2008

Page 1: Sand dunes, Water Canyon, Santa Rosa Island.
Pages 2-3: Inspiration Point, Anacapa Island.

A special note of appreciation to NASA/GSFC/LaRC/JPL, MISR Team, for use of the satellite image on page 13

Rainbow Bridge

The first Chumash people were created on Santa Cruz Island. They were made from the seeds of a magic plant by an earth goddess named Hutash.

Hutash was married to Sky Snake, the Milky Way. Sky Snake could make lightning bolts with his tongue. One day he sent down a bolt of lightning that started a fire. It scared the people, then they were glad. Now they could stay warm and cook their food.

The presence of fire enabled the Chumash to live more comfortably. Each year they had more babies, and their villages got bigger and bigger. So many people talking and squalling! The racket kept Hutash awake at night.

She decided that some of the Chumash would have to move off the island and go to the mainland, where few people lived in those days. But how were the people to get across the water? Hutash wove an iridescent bridge out of the drops of a rainbow—a very long, very high rainbow that stretched from the tallest mountain on Santa Cruz Island all the way to the tallest mountain on the mainland.

The Chumash started across the bridge. Some got across safely; others made the mistake of looking down into the swirling fog. They got so dizzy that some of them fell off the bridge. Hutash felt badly about that. She didn't want them to drown, so she turned them into dolphins. To this day the Chumash claim the dolphins are their brothers.

CHUMASH LEGEND

Contents

INTRODUCTION 11

Anacapa Island

19

Santa Cruz Island

43

Santa Rosa Island

73

San Miguel Island

97

Santa Barbara Island

123

National Marine Sanctuary

141

APPENDIX 158

BIBLIOGRAPHY 159

Skunk Point, Santa Rosa Island,
with Santa Cruz Island in the background.

INTRODUCTION
WORLDS APART

At first glance it seems as if sizable chunks of the mainland have flaked off the coast of Southern California and floated a short distance out to sea. On a clear day, from a point high in the Santa Ynez Mountains behind the city of Santa Barbara, the four northern islands of Channel Islands National Park—Anacapa, Santa Cruz, Santa Rosa, and San Miguel—are plainly visible. The fifth, tiny Santa Barbara Island, barely a mile square and sixty-two nautical miles away, can also be seen.

The four northern islands range single file from east to west, parallel to the coast like a flotilla of mismatched ships. Geologically, over many millions of years, the islands were formed by a combination of volcanic activity, fluctuating sea levels, and shifting plate tectonics. Paleomagnetic examination of rocks from the northern Channel Islands and the Transverse Range indicates that they rest on a long sliver of the earth's crust that has rotated about eighty-five degrees from its original position. Certain rocks from San Miguel Island match certain rocks from the San Diego region, suggesting they may once have been neighbors.

Around 24 million years ago, lava and ash flows spewed and rumbled throughout the region. The Pacific Plate slid past the North American Plate along a network of faults, creating a clockwise rotation that continues to push the Channel Islands closer to the mainland at the rate of around six millimeters a year.

The Continental Borderland, as the area between the California Channel Islands and the mainland is called, is one of the most complex and varied stretches of undersea topography anywhere on the planet. Deep channels separate the islands from both the mainland and each other. Their adjacent position along the edge of the North American continent classifies them as "fringe islands." The floor between the islands and the mainland is filled with sea mounts, basins, escarpments, and submarine canyons. Portions of this complex borderland date back as far as 100 million years B.P.

At the onset of the Ice Age, about 5.2 million years B.P., ocean levels dropped as more and more water became locked up in the expanding polar icecaps. Much later, as the icecaps melted and the sea levels rose again, marine terraces appeared along the edges of the islands and the California coast.

A once popular theory suggested that the islands were linked to the mainland by a land bridge. Today, most marine biologists believe that less than 20,000 years ago, the four northern Channel Islands formed one gigantic super-island. As the Ice Age wound down and the glaciers drained into the sea, this huge island, called Santarosae, broke up into a series of islands. Around 12,000 years ago, Santa Cruz and Anacapa separated. Within the next 2,000 years San Miguel appeared. Since then, the islands have gradually shrunk to their present size and are likely to keep shrinking as the sea continues to rise and the waves wash against the shores.

It is now believed that prehistoric mammoths swam to the islands, where they soon found themselves isolated. Unable for whatever reason to swim back to the mainland, they adapted to the limited resources of island life by growing smaller and smaller until they were barely five feet high. The last mammoths are thought to have died out about 12,000 years ago. Their fossilized remains have been discovered on San Miguel, Santa Rosa, Santa Cruz, and San Nicolas islands.

Human settlement of the islands began over 13,000 years ago. The word Canaliño, meaning "channel people," refers to all the Channel Islands native peoples. The Gabrielino occupied the southern Channel Islands—Santa Catalina, San Nicolas, San Clemente, Santa Barbara—the Chumash the northern Channel Islands—Anacapa, Santa Cruz, Santa Rosa, San Miguel.

The Chumash were one of the most complex and sophisticated native cultures in North America. They lived in harmony with a world whose natural features provided them with just about everything they needed. Food was never a pressing problem, as they had the best of both worlds, terrestrial and marine. They gathered acorns and nuts; from the nearby sea they took a variety of fish, mammals, and shellfish. They also basked in the glow of a benign climate that blessed them with mild winters and comfortable summers. On the mainland their territory stretched from Point Conception, along the foothills of the coastal region, all the way to the Santa Monica Mountains and the Los Angeles Basin; it also included the Santa Barbara Channel and the four islands that border the channel to the south.

The Chumash cosmogony was composed of three separate worlds. The world they occupied was in the middle. That world was circular and flat, forming a large island that floated on top of the water. Dangerous monsters dwelled in the world directly below, while Sun and Moon lived in the world above. Two giant snakes held up the middle world from underneath. When the snakes grew restless, the earth trembled and quaked. An eagle held up the upper world. When he got tired he stretched his wings, which caused the phases of the moon. The eagle could also blot out the moon by covering it with his wings.

Left: Spring rains transform the slopes of North Peak into a garden paradise, Santa Barbara Island.

Opposite page: Satellite view of the Channel Islands.

The Island Chumash developed their own dialect and culture, distinct from the Mainland Chumash. They were adroit hunters and gatherers, making use of the many food and material resources they found on both land and sea, from seeds and nuts to gigantic whales that washed up onshore. Thousands of middens—mounds of shell and fish fragments—are found throughout the islands, remnants of both temporary and long-term habitats.

The Chumash traveled widely in twenty-foot-long wood-plank canoes called tomols, handcrafted out of slabs of redwood, sewn together with milkweed cord, sealed along the seams with a mix of pine pitch and asphalt. They traded pelts, dried fish, obsidian, and other hard stones; their primary medium of exchange was a form of bead money made out of of iridescent Olivella shells, perforated and strung on leather thongs.

One of the most exciting moments for the members of an island village was the arrival of a tomol from the mainland. Eleanor Hoffmann described it in her book *The Charmstone* (1981): "To skim across the dark blue ocean with the paddles flying in rhythm, to see strange faces, above all to trade cunningly with these strangers and return the richer, that was the keen delight of everyone from the old grandfathers to the boys."

Not so exciting was the arrival to the islands in the sixteenth, seventeenth, and eighteenth centuries of Spanish explorers such as Juan Rodriguez Cabrillo, Sebastian Vizcaino, and Gaspar de Portola. They were looking for gold, but there was none to be found on these tranquil islands riding just within eyeshot of the California coastline. The Spanish claimed the islands anyway; by the early nineteenth century, Russian mariners were making their way down the Pacific Coast from Alaska in search of another form of gold: the deep, lustrous pelts of the sea otter. Otter furs found their way onboard Manila galleons to Asia, where they were more highly prized than fox or sable. Stimulated by the demand, the Russians, along with their Aleut Indian allies, scoured the California coast, threatening the animals with extinction. Today, the majority of extant sea otters are found north of Point Conception on the California mainland, with a few occasionally sighted around Channel Islands National Park.

The Chumash when the Spanish appeared were living in large domed houses with thatched roofs. "The Indians of these islands are very poor," sniffed Juan Rodriguez Cabrillo in 1542. "They are fishermen; they eat nothing but fish; they sleep on the ground; their sole business and employment is to fish. They say that in each house there are fifty souls. They live very swinishly and go about naked."

Accompanying the explorers was the usual contingent of Franciscan friars—pale, cadaverous, humorless devotees of the Roman Catholic faith—in search of pagan souls to convert. Christianity was not the only gift of dubious value the Spanish introduced to the indigenous people of California; diseases such as measles, cholera, and smallpox—unknown in the New World—wreaked havoc on the native population. By the early 1800s, disease and famine (this in a land so bounteously blessed with sources of food) had decimated the health of the islanders; the last remaining few were finally removed to the mainland in the 1820s.

When Mexico gained independence from Spain in 1821, the Channel Islands became part of the new Republic of Mexico. Three islands—Santa Cruz, Santa Rosa, and Santa Catalina—were deeded over to private owners. In 1848 the Treaty of Guadalupe Hidalgo ceded California and the Channel Islands to the United States.

Each island has its own history and specialty. Each island offers something different to savor and enjoy. Each island has its stalwart defenders. But the cumulative experience is the same. No one returns to the mainland after spending time out there without feeling significantly changed for the better.

It's taken more than forty years to finally bring all five islands into the protective orbit of The National Park Service and The Nature Conservancy. The road along the way has been bumpy and contentious at times, but the prize is well worth it.

In 1938, two islands, Santa Barbara and Anacapa, were decreed a national monument with a stroke of the pen by President Franklin Roosevelt. Creating a national park is a more complex process, involving the cooperation of the people in the region and the participation of the U.S. Congress. By 1980, as a result of the dedicated skill and diplomacy of all the factions involved, San Miguel, Santa Rosa, and portions of Santa Cruz Island obtained national park status. This new national park included one mile of water around each island, which in total area places half of the park underwater. By 1998 the myriad pieces of the Channel Islands mosaic were finally put into place.

Opposite page, top: Endangered snowy plover, Santa Rosa Island.

Opposite page, bottom: California gray whale.

Above: A northerly view from Montañon Ridge, Santa Cruz Island.

Also in 1980, in recognition of the significant marine life and resources around the Channel Islands, the waters within six nautical miles of the four northern Channel Islands and Santa Barbara Island were declared a National Marine Sanctuary. This designation includes about 1,128 square nautical miles of habitat, which is administered by the National Oceanic and Atmospheric Administration (NOAA). Today the park, together with the National Marine Sanctuary, offers visitors an unprecedented opportunity to observe rare and endangered wildlife, on land and at sea, in an open and natural setting.

Some sixty-five plants are endemic to the Channel Islands, including island ironwood, island cherry, island oaks, manzanita, buckwheat, and live-forever (*dudleya*). Some of the most common endemic animals include the island fox, spotted skunk, and deer mouse. The islands are also a bird-watcher's paradise, providing a home for hundreds of land and marine species. The nesting sites of the California brown pelican, Xantus' murrelet, western gull, and others enjoy special protection.

Perhaps the best-known mammals found on and around the islands today are the pinnipeds—California sea lions, harbor seals, Northern fur seals, and Northern elephant seals. The spectacle of thousands of these creatures congregating at the islands' breeding sites is one of the most astounding events in all of the natural world.

Opposite page: McMinn's Manzanita blossom, Santa Cruz Island.

Above: Westerly view from Montañon Ridge, Santa Cruz Island.

Inspiration Point.

Anacapa Island
ENDLESS ILLUSION

You see it all the way out across the Santa Barbara Channel as the boat plows across the lacy-white waves stirred up by the steady wind. Scaly, dry, beguiling, the island rises through the water like a basking lizard. At least that's the way it looks at a distance. Up close, it's actually broken into three segments—East, Middle, and West Anacapa. *"Las Mesitas,"* early Spanish explorers called them, "little tables" that vary in size and height.

The name of the island derives from a word in the Chumash language, Anyapak, meaning "mirage" or "ever-changing." An apt description of the chimerical presence of the island, the way it appears and disappears through the scrolls of fog and mist that billow off the Santa Barbara Channel. Though only eleven miles from the mainland, there's something mysterious about the place, something isolated and otherworldly.

Visitors go ashore at the landing site on East Anacapa Island, where they scale a vertical stairway of 154 steps to reach the island's top shelf (200 feet above sea level). Once there, an enchanting world opens up. An easy ramble along the island's two miles of hiking trails pretty much takes them everywhere they need to go. Part of the trail meanders through a large western gull rookery; between April and July, there are either eggs or young gulls around, requiring visitors to watch carefully where they step. The trail stops at Inspiration Point, which offers dramatic views of Middle Anacapa and West Anacapa.

Spring flowers, particularly the stunning coreopsis—a bizarre-looking member of the sunflower family, whose brown, lifeless stalks erupt into bright yellow blossoms in late winter and early spring—dazzle the eye. The panoramic views out to sea and back toward the mainland are spectacular. The wind blows incessantly. Two other sounds predominate—the steady slap of waves against the eroded base of the island, and the blasting moan of the foghorn on the Anacapa lighthouse.

Juan Rodriguez Cabrillo sailed past here in 1542, but neither he nor any other Spanish explorer reported signs of habitation. The shortage of freshwater forced the Chumash Indians to occupy Anacapa Island seasonally rather than in permanent settlements. Indian Water Cave, on West Anacapa Island just west of Frenchy's Cove, contains the island's only source of freshwater, a slow drip from the cave's vaulted ceiling that pings into a hollow rock basin, producing two or three quarts of brackish water in twenty-four hours.

Between 1902 and 1937, four different groups of people leased the island, most notably H. Bayfield Webster, who raised sheep and ran a fishing concession. In 1938 President Franklin Roosevelt conferred national monument status on Anacapa and Santa Barbara islands. In 1970 Anacapa Island came under the jurisdiction of The National Park Service.

The legendary Raymond LeDreau, a.k.a. "Frenchy," originally from Brittany, consoled himself for his failure to become a cleric by sailing all over the world. Reportedly, he joined the U.S. Navy and fought in the Spanish-American War. While on leave in California, he married a woman named Emma, by whom he fathered three children. She died in 1918 of the flu epidemic; grief-stricken, Frenchy decided to retire from the world. Nearby Anacapa—so close and yet so far—seemed a fortuitous choice.

For nearly three decades he rarely left the island, functioning as a kind of unofficial greeter, preferring to trade the catch he pulled from the sea for containers of wine and water people from the mainland brought him on the weekends. Always gallant with the ladies, Frenchy serenaded them with romantic songs in a sweet tenor voice. He liked to tell sea stories and engage in deep discussions about his favorite works of literature. In 1954, at age eighty—after twenty-six years on the island—he injured himself in a bad fall on the sharp rocks and was taken to the mainland for treatment.

The three small islets that make up Anacapa Island—East, Middle, and West Anacapa—are cut off from one another except at the lowest tides. Taken together, the cumulative area covers just 1.1 square miles, making Anacapa the second smallest of the Channel Islands, after Santa Barbara Island.

East Anacapa sunrise.

Cathedral Cove.

At first glance, East Anacapa appears inaccessible. It rises out of the sea, squat and stolid, like a medieval fortress, with no apparent access to the top. And then, as the boat nears the eastern tip, flocks of birds appear, along with the 154 steps. In truth, East Anacapa is one of the most visited spots on the Channel Islands; because of its proximity to the mainland (eleven miles), it's the day-tripper's favorite destination.

Swimmers cool off at Landing Cove on calm summer days. Boaters drop anchor at nearby Cathedral Cove, with its unusual volcanic formations. Cathedral Cave, a multi-chamber sea cave, can be explored by skiff or kayak. Just beyond East Anacapa, water erosion has carved a famous local landmark called Arch Rock, a forty-foot-high natural arch famed artist James Whistler first pictured on an engraving in 1854.

Middle Anacapa is three miles long yet seldom more than an eighth of a mile wide; it's best known as the site of a famous shipwreck. In 1853 the paddlewheel steamer *Winfield Scott* ran aground and sank here with 150 passengers onboard; miraculously, there was no loss of life.

West Anacapa, the largest of the three islets, also has the greatest topographical diversity. At 930 feet, Summit Peak is the highest point on Anacapa Island. The beach at Frenchy's Cove is popular with boat-borne visitors. At low tide, it's possible to walk from Frenchy's Cove to the south side of the island, which offers exceptional tide pools. Public access to West Anacapa is restricted to Frenchy's Cove and the tide-pool area to protect the West Coast's primary nesting site of endangered California brown pelicans.

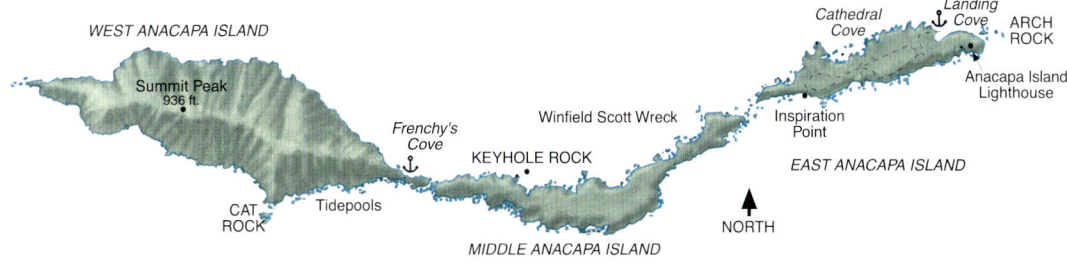

ANACAPA ISLAND   21

Opposite page: Indian paintbrush.

Above: Impressive displays of wildflowers cover East Anacapa Island following winter rains.

Previous spread: One of the most awe-inspiring views in Channel Islands National Park is this sweeping vista from Inspiration Point.

Opposite page: The Californian sails past forty-foot-high Arch Rock.

Above: Early morning light on Arch Rock.

During early summer, island cliff-astor accents the trail leading to the lighthouse.

The current lighthouse, built in 1932, became fully automated in 1967.

Ocean kayakers set off to explore some of Anacapa's 135 charted sea caves.

Middle Anacapa.

A springtime display of coreopsis at Inspiration Point.

Left: Inspiration Point.

Above: Wind, water, and waves have eroded Anacapa's volcanic rock into steep cliffs and interesting arches such as Keyhole Rock.

ANACAPA ISLAND 35

Opposite page: Green sea anemones and countless other marine creatures dwell in the tide pools near Frenchy's Cove.

Above: Forests of giant bladder kelp, such as this one on the south side of Middle Anacapa, support a diverse community of marine life.

Craggy rocks and isolated beaches such as these on the south side of of Anacapa Island (above) or near arch rock (opposite page) are important haul-out spots and rookery sites for harbor seals and California sea lions.

And yet we have all known flights when all of a sudden, each for himself, it has seemed to us that we have crossed the border of the world of reality; when only a couple of hours from port, we have felt ourselves more distant from it than we should feel if we were in India; when there has come a premonition of an incursion into a forbidden world whence it was going to be infinitely difficult to return.

ANTOINE DE SAINT EXUPERY
Wind, Sand and Stars (1939)

40 CHANNEL ISLANDS

Opposite page: California brown pelican. West Anacapa is the primary California brown pelican rookery on the West Coast of North America.

Above: Over 10,000 western gulls gather for nesting on Anacapa Island during the spring and summer.

SANTA CRUZ ISLAND
CROWN JEWEL

Santa Cruz Island is the crown jewel in the diadem of offshore islands that make up Channel Islands National Park. At ninety-six square miles, it's the biggest island in the park, with its own history and allure. For years, under the guidance of different families, the island served as a working ranch for the production of sheep and cattle. Today, protection and preservation of island resources are divided between The Nature Conservancy, which owns and manages the western 76 percent of the island, and The National Park Service, which owns and operates the eastern 24 percent.

The National Park section of the island is the place most people visit. Two maritime franchise services run regular trips year-round from the California mainland to two ports of call on the Park Service side: Prisoners Harbor and Scorpion Anchorage. The coastline between the two landing sites is pocked and scalloped with unspoiled coves and beaches, which offer cozy havens for private boats.

Goldfields brighten Smuggler's Field below Montañon Ridge.

Santa Cruz Island is a feast for the senses. Arriving by boat on a warm summer day can ignite the imagination. In the lee of Prisoners Harbor the water calms down and the boat, safely out of the choppy swell of the Santa Barbara Channel, stops pitching. Massive hills, grooved and rounded, their smooth, grassy slopes glowing in the midday sun, rise out of the sea like the tawny backs of basking sea lions. Live oaks glisten in dark clusters down in the draws and hollows, along with the scaly red bark of the gnarly chaparral. The wind that luffs across the harbor brings the licorice scent of sun-drenched fennels.

From the mouth of a stream that trickles into Prisoners Harbor, a dirt road winds up through sere-colored hills to the ridge that dominates the neck of the island on the Park Service side. The view from the top encompasses a panorama of the sea in every direction. A brisk wind sweeps over the slopes, stirring the dry grass. Doves arc over the hillsides as if catapulted from slingshots. A redtailed hawk hovers on whisking wings. Ravens croak and gurgle as they lumber into the wind.

Also from this vantage point, looking to the west, the Central Valley can be seen, running through the heart of The Nature Conservancy portion of the island. The valley is a geological fault line that divides two impressive mountain ranges, each rising over 2,000 feet, that border the north and south coasts. The highest point on the island, Picacho Diablo, at 2,450 feet, is located in the north range. To the east looms Montañon Ridge, capped by Montañon Peak, at 1,808 feet the highest point on the Park Service side and a popular destination for energetic hikers.

Islands recapitulate in miniature many of the features of the larger bodies they are adjacent to, and this is certainly true of Santa Cruz Island, which resembles mainland California in flora, fauna, and geology. Although visitation is restricted on The Nature Conservancy side of the island, a stroll through the spacious Central Valley or anywhere else on the island is like a trip back in time to when California was a bucolic paradise—no freeways, traffic, or shopping malls.

Some of the oldest and tallest blue-gum eucalyptus trees in California are found in the Central Valley. The exotic tree, originally from Australia, was first planted on the island in the 1880s. Today, as in the past, the wind soughing through the messy, splintered branches grinds them together with an eerie groan curiously reminscent of the calls gray whales make to one another out in the Santa Barbara Channel.

Scorpion Anchorage, near the eastern tip, is the main jumping-off spot for visiting Santa Cruz Island. Swimming, snorkeling, and scuba diving are popular activities in and around the anchorage, along with kayaking. Scorpion Ranch House, built in the 1880s, has been refurbished; of special interest is the built-in bake oven, which supplied fresh bread to the French and Italian workers who came to the island in the late nineteenth and early twentieth centuries to herd cattle and shear sheep and harvest grapes. Today, visitors come for the scenery, the solitude, the flowers, the birds, the hiking.

Those with plenty of time start up the trail that winds over a soaring marine terrace and down through an olive grove to Smuggler's Cove—a strenuous three-hour hike—to an old stone farmhouse nestled in a canyon near a smooth white beach. Here, amid the lap of waves and the swaying of tall trees, the past seems palpably alive.

Chumash Indians and their ancestors lived on the island for at least 11,000 years; remnants of their middens and villages are scattered everywhere. Island Chumash called Santa Cruz Limuw, "in the sea." Mainland Chumash called it Michumash, "place of the islanders." Spanish explorers in the eighteenth century found upwards of 2,000 inhabitants living on the island in at least a dozen villages. During the Portola expedition of 1769, a Franciscan priest misplaced a staff tipped with an iron cross. The Chumash returned it the next day—hence the name Isla de la Santa Cruz: "Island of the Holy Cross."

The trail over Montañon Ridge is steep and rugged.

Scorpion Anchorage.

In 1807 a measles epidemic killed off hundreds of Chumash, prompting the survivors to move to the mainland. In 1839 the Mexican governor granted ownership of Santa Cruz to Andres Castillero, who over the next eighteen years established one of the most successful sheep operations in California.

In 1869 ownership passed to a group of ten investors from San Francisco. One of these men, Justinian Caire, ultimately acquired all the stock in the corporation and developed a variety of agricultural and ranching ventures on the island.

Caire raised sheep and cattle and grew hay and alfalfa. He also planted over 200 acres of grapevines. Two large brick buildings that housed the winery, as well as a chapel and other Central Valley ranch structures, are still used today by The Nature Conservancy and the Santa Cruz Island Foundation.

The habitat of Santa Cruz Island is the most diverse of any island in the park. Endemic plants include island lace pod, island manzanita, silver lotus, island mallow, gooseberry, and monkey flower. The Santa Cruz Island jay, found on no other island, is 25 percent larger than its mainland counterpart, a phenomenon known as "island gigantism." Lack of competition and predators allowed this island species to utilize resources generally unavailable to mainland jays.

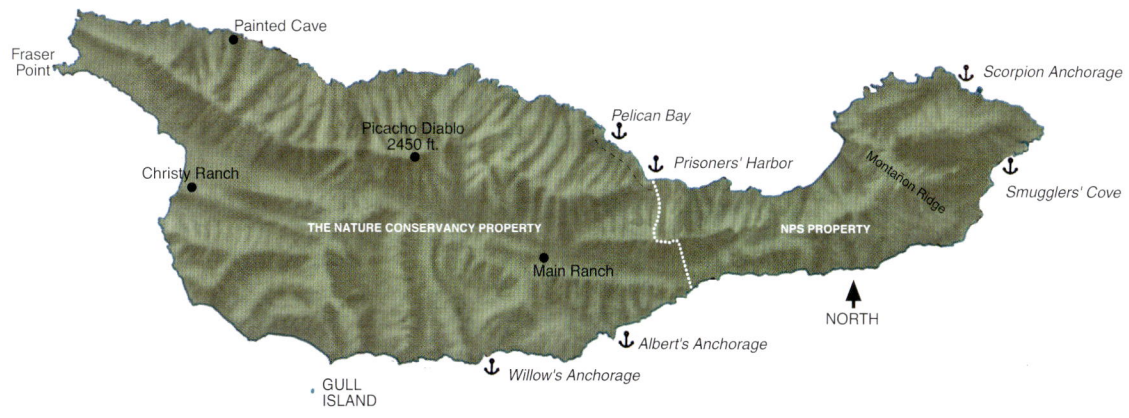

Previous spread: Scorpion Anchorage and historic Scorpion Ranch.

Opposite page: View from Potato Harbor trail.

Above: Cavern Point panorama.

Previous spread: The strenuous Scorpion Canyon Trail opens onto a grassy plateau on the way to Montañon Ridge.

Opposite page: A wide sandy beach and a historic olive grove welcome visitors to Smuggler's Cove.

Above: This westerly view from the top of Montañon Ridge reveals the rugged topography of Santa Cruz Island.

Previous spread: Remnants of the island's ranching era near Smuggler's Field.

Above: One of the best hiking trails on Santa Cruz Island is between Prisoners Harbor and Pelican Bay.

Numerous picturesque anchorages such as this one at Forney's Cove, near the west end of the island, offer refuge to boaters.

Above: Sunrise view of Anacapa Island from the island's isthmus.

Opposite page: Bush monkey flower.

SANTA CRUZ ISLAND

Pelican Bay.

Ever since I had come back from Pelican Bay [Santa Cruz Island], I had been so restless. I always had the feeling that I wanted to start right back to the islands—something over there just drew me to them.

MARGARET HOLDEN EATON
Diary of a Sea Captain's Wife (1980)

I never saw such beauty in the animal world. Really, the chesnut reds, bluish grays and black of this smallest of the foxes formed a strikingly beautiful combination. He was certainly splendid, and we got very close to him. I suppose the closest was when he came toward us; we thought he was going to be actually affectionate like a cat as he must have come within 8 or 10 feet.

WILLIAM OBERLIN DAWSON
Diary Kept While on Santa Cruz Island (1919).
A Step Back in Time, edited by Marla Daily (1990)

Above left: Santa Cruz Island jay.

Above right: Santa Cruz Island fox.

Both are endemic to the island.

Opposite page: Santa Cruz Island ironwood.

64 CHANNEL ISLANDS

As night came on, the wild influence of Nature, the barking of the sea lions, and the dashing of the waves on the beach impressed us with a great sense of the remoteness and solitude of the place; but there was a wonderful beauty in the scene, as both the sea and shore were lighted by the moon, which was hidden from us by the overhanging, towering crags.

EUNICE FELTON
Camping on Santa Cruz Island
A Step Back in Time, edited by Marla Daily (1990)

Opposite page top: Chinese Harbor.

Opposite page bottom: Del Norte Ranch.

Above: A full moon settles across The Nature Conservancy portion of the island, as seen from the isthmus.

Left: The Santa Cruz Island fault running through the Central Valley, splits the island into two mountain ridges with volcanic rock on the north ridge and older sedimentary rock on the south.

Above: The island bush poppy is endemic to Santa Cruz Island.

Chapel interior.

Built with island-made brick in 1891, the chapel is part of the historic Main Ranch in the Central Valley.

Early morning light illuminates a magnificent island big-pod ceanothus on the island's isthmus.

Sunrise, Scorpion Anchorage.

SANTA ROSA ISLAND
OLD CALIFORNIA

The image is a part of the island's history and lore.

For nearly a hundred years Santa Rosa was a cowboy island, a pastoral grazing range for premier beef cattle. Mexican *vaqueros* conducted roundups every year, bringing the cattle down from the surrounding pastures and hills and driving them out onto the pier at Bechers Bay, where they were loaded onto a wood-hulled boat and transported to the mainland.

The Smith Highway.

The *vaqueros,* wearing dusty leather chaps, wool shirts, baseball caps with obscure logos, jingling spurs with spiky pinwheel rowls, sat erect in their saddles, backs straight, clutching the thin, fibrous stems of snap whips they flicked with surgical precision against the buttocks of the bawling steers.

All that began to wind down in 1986 when The National Park Service assumed ownership of the island while permitting Vail & Vickers, the island's proprietors since 1902, to graze cattle under a special use permit until 1998.

The topography of Santa Rosa Island—second largest island in Channel Islands National Park, fifteen miles long by ten miles wide—alternates between wide, grassy slopes and steep, rugged canyons. The coastline is rimmed with smooth marine terraces, stark cliffs, isolated beaches, and pristine tide pools. The Chumash called the island Wima: "driftwood." Attracted by plentiful food and clear, freshwater springs and streams, sizable populations of Chumash settled here at least a millennium ago; to date, several thousand archaeological sites have been identified.

The Chumash called the sun Kakunupmawa. A major festival took place at the time of the winter solstice on Santa Rosa Island. An old man *(paha),* aided by helpers, erected a sunstick about a foot and a half tall in the center of a patch of ceremonial ground. The incised and perforated stone atop the sunstick was painted green or blue to resemble a sand dollar.

The Chumash believed the sand dollar represented the sun. As the sun rolls across the sky during the day, it stops and rests, ducking for cover in the holes of the sand dollar. To release the power of the sunstick, the paha tapped the stone and sang sacred songs; he then pulled the stick (and, symbolically, the sun) in a northward direction, so it would shine directly on the islands.

Thousands of years ago, Santa Rosa Island was home to prehistoric mammoths. More mammoth fossils have been uncovered here than on any other Channel Island. In 1994 archaeologists excavated the most complete skeleton ever found of a rare pygmy mammoth, dating back 12,000 years. The rich Pleistocene fossil beds on the north side of the island reveal the presence of other creatures such as giant mice, flightless geese, and vampire bats.

A severe earthquake in 1812, which destroyed the Santa Barbara Mission on the mainland, had its epicenter close to Santa Rosa Island. A massive rift opened on the island near Lobo Canyon—1,000 feet long, 100 feet wide, and 50 feet deep. The destruction was terrible and may have convinced the remaining Chumash to depart for the mainland.

The 1840s and 1850s were the halcyon days of old Spanish California, when the island was a cattle ranchería. From 1858 to 1902, the More brothers converted the operation to a sheep ranch, which proved profitable, especially during the Civil War when wool for military uniforms was in great demand. In 1902 Walter Vail and J. V. Vickers bought the ranch from the heirs of A. P. More and turned it back into a cattle operation.

Torrey pine, Bechers Bay.

Not far from the main ranch on Bechers Bay, a stand of Torrey pines grows at elevations of 200-500 feet—the only native Torrey pines on the Channel Islands. (Torrey pines occur naturally at only one other location, on the Southern California coast just south of Del Mar in San Diego County.)

Bishop pine forests, relicts from the Pleistocene Age, can be found at slightly higher altitudes on the island. Twelve groves of endemic island oaks dot the grassy hillsides. Elk and deer, introduced to Santa Rosa as game animals in the early 1900s, are still hunted today. Native mammals include the island fox, deer mouse, and spotted skunk.

Santa Rosa's coastline varies from spectacular beaches to rocky rims pocked with tide pools. Harbor seals, elephant seals, and sea lions haul out on any open space they can find. A rare coastal marsh at the island's eastern end forms the most extensive freshwater habitat on the Channel Islands. Together, the island's grasslands and marshlands support over 195 species of land and marine birds, from European starlings to Brandt's cormorants.

Numerous shipwrecks surround Santa Rosa Island. The *Chickasaw*, a freighter en route from Japan in 1962 with a cargo of toys and optical supplies, ran aground on the south side of the island; sizable sections of the shattered hull remain exposed today.

With the landscape recovering from the impact of nearly 150 years of sheep and cattle grazing, backpackers are enjoying the hilly terrain with its sweeping vistas. Choice spots include the two-mile stretch of unspoiled beach near the campground at Water Canyon, the spectacular beach and sea caves at Southeast Anchorage, and the unique sculptured sandstone formations at Lobo Canyon.

Sandy Point at the west end of the island is dotted with pristine tide pools crammed with organisms: keyhole limpets, hermit crabs, acorn and gooseneck barnacles, bristly sea urchins, sculpins, orange sea stars, gaping anemones, limber strands of eelgrass.

Mexican *vaqueros* often fashioned their own rope, saddles, and bridles.

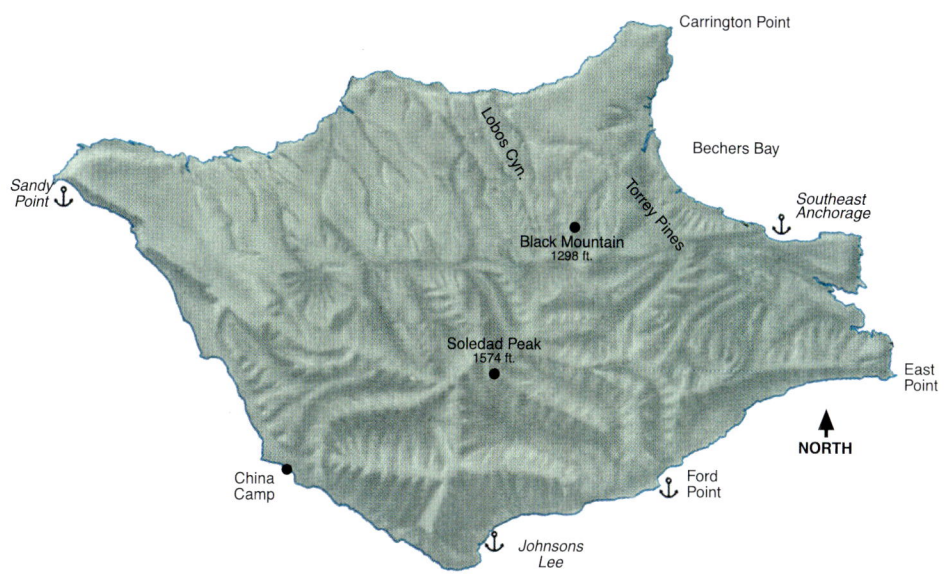

SANTA ROSA ISLAND

Previous spread: Diverse marine ecosystems such as this one near the mouth of Lobo Canyon support a wide array of life.

Above: Mouth of Lobo Canyon.

Opposite page: Munchkin dudleya, a flower endemic to East Point, flowers in early summer.

On these remote bits of earth, nature has excelled in the creation of strange and wonderful forms. As though to prove her incredible versatility, almost every island has developed species that are endemic—that is, they are peculiar to it alone and are duplicated nowhere else on earth.

RACHEL CARSON
The Sea Around Us (1954)

Above: Arlington Canyon.

Opposite page: A year-round stream flows through Acapulco Canyon.

Previous spread: Freshwater marsh, near East Point.

Opposite page: Badlands topography on the western end of Santa Rosa Island.

Above: Water and wind erosion have carved the sandstone walls of Lobo Canyon.

Opposite page: Carrington Point.

Above: Southeast Anchorage.

Previous spread: Sandy Point is only three miles from San Miguel Island, seen here in the distance.

Above: East Point.

Strong northwesterly winds have shaped and sifted the fine-grained white sand dunes at China Camp beach.

Above: Built in the 1870s, the main ranch house at Bechers Bay is on the National Register of Historic Places.

Opposite page: Rustic corrals are reminiscent of Santa Rosa's colorful ranching history.

Following spread: Evening light settles on Santa Rosa Island.

I've been out here just about fifty years. Well, once you get out here, it's damned hard to find a reason to ever go back. I only get into town when I absolutley have to. That's about once or twice a year, and that's too goddamned much.

Gretel Ehrlich (2000)
Bill Wallace, quoted in *Cowboy Island*

San Miguel Island
PINNIPEDS AND CALICHE

San Miguel, the westernmost of the five islands that make up Channel Islands National Park, is the one most directly exposed to the wild weather that rolls in undeflected from the Pacific Ocean. A glance at the map reveals the situation—San Miguel is like the lead ship of a stationary squadron lined up alongside the coast of Southern California. Because of its exposed position at the head of the formation, the weather on the island is chronically foul. Rain, wind, days of muffling fog alternate with a few cloudless periods when the sun beams and the waves splashing ashore at Cuyler Harbor glow with a warm, appealing light. Submerged rocks and shoals pose an extreme hazard for boats in the region; so many shipwrecks have occurred that San Miguel has come to be known as "the graveyard of the Pacific."

Harris Point.

From the air the surface of the undulating, fourteen-square-mile island looks as if it has been raked by the claws of a giant bear. No other island exhibits the same wind-ravaged face. The degree of its exposure to the winds that blast past Point Conception is partly responsible for the gouging; additionally, sheep ranching and overgrazing in the nineteenth and twentieth centuries took a terrible toll on the native flora and fauna.

From 1850 to 1948, stockmen from the mainland raised sheep and a few cattle on the limited stands of arable grass growing in the swales between the rolling dunes. Early pioneer George Nidever was the first to begin ranching on San Miguel in 1852. Two other prominent figures from this entrepreneurial era are Captain William G. Waters, who conducted wool-growing operations from 1887 to 1917, and Robert Brooks, who maintained grazing leases from 1917 to 1948. Between 1930 and 1942, Herbert Lester—a colorful character known as "the King of San Miguel"—managed the island for Brooks.

Elizabeth Sherman Lester, Herbert's wife, left a fascinating memoir of the twelve years (1930–1942) the Lester family (they had two daughters) spent on San Miguel Island. Herbert Lester, a shell-shocked veteran of World War I, was hired by Brooks to manage the island in Brooks's absence. Life was heartachingly lonely at times. The girls were homeschooled. The wind blew incessantly. Fog shrouded the island. Twice a year, relief was provided by parties of Mexican workers who came ashore to shear the wool off the herds of Rambouillet sheep.

Meanwhile, on the mainland, the nation was mired in the worst economic depression in its history, but all that seemed dim and distant to the island-bound Lesters. With no radio and few newspapers to peruse, the family remained out of touch. Varmints such as the vexatious sand flea preoccupied their attention. "Of all the pestiferous nuisances we lived with from time to time on San Miguel," wrote Elizabeth Lester, "the fleas, everlasting and abiding without lag, won the honor of being the most obnoxious."

By the late 1970s, all the feral sheep and burros had been removed from the island. Since then, the recovery of the plant life—coreopsis, dudleya, locoweed, lupine, buckwheat, coastal sagebrush—has been dramatic. The return of these native species has helped stabilize the ravaged soil against the destructive winds.

Only two terrestrial mammals, the island fox and the deer mouse, are known to inhabit San Miguel Island. Archaeological evidence indicates that ornate shrews and the spotted skunk once lived on the island.

Most intriguing are the remnants of the tusks of two Pleistocine-era elephants, first discovered by Herbert Lester in 1932, lying exposed on a cliff top where the animals, locked in combat, had evidently dueled to the death. Representatives from the Santa Barbara Museum of Natural History came to the island to see for themselves. They went back to the mainland full of stories about the historic find but failed to credit Herbert Lester's pivotal role in locating the artifacts. Lester was further miffed when, on a trip to the mainland, he found that the tusks had been sequestered in a musty room in the depths of the museum.

The Chumash called the island Tuqan, a name that has no known translation. Radiocarbon dating indicates that Native Americans inhabited San Miguel as long as 11,600 years ago; over 600 archaeolgical sites have been identified.

Cuyler Point with Prince Island in the background.

In 1542, explorer Juan Rodriguez Cabrillo became the first European to land on San Miguel Island. According to legend, it also may be his final resting place. Cabrillo sustained injuries, possibly a broken arm or leg, when he fell out of his skiff while coming ashore and he died of a subsequent infection in the winter of 1543. Though his grave was never found, a monument honoring him was placed above Cuyler Harbor in 1937.

Two fascinating natural attractions draw visitors to San Miguel Island. Huge colonies of seals and sea lions lumber ashore every year at Point Bennett on the western end of the island to breed and give birth. A sixteen-mile round-trip trail leads to an overlook where the saturnalia can be observed. Of the six species of pinnipeds that have been known to use this sandy peninsula—California sea lion, Steller sea lion, northern fur seal, Guadalupe fur seal, northern elephant seal, and harbor seal—all except the Steller sea lion and the Guadalupe fur seal are common and breed here.

It's damp and chilly on San Miguel Island in January. Fog scrolls in from the sea, obscuring the headlands, the animals milling about onshore. A misty wind sweeps in from the west, muffling the rolling terrain. Thousands of years ago the thin soil supported a population of trees. Sheets of wind-borne sand cloaked the trunks and limbs with grainy castings of calcium carbonate. Eventually, the trees suffocated. Clusters of fossilized roots and stumps, chalk-white fields of twisted remnants, spectral and eerie—the caliche ghost forest—are all that remain today.

Cabrillo Monument.

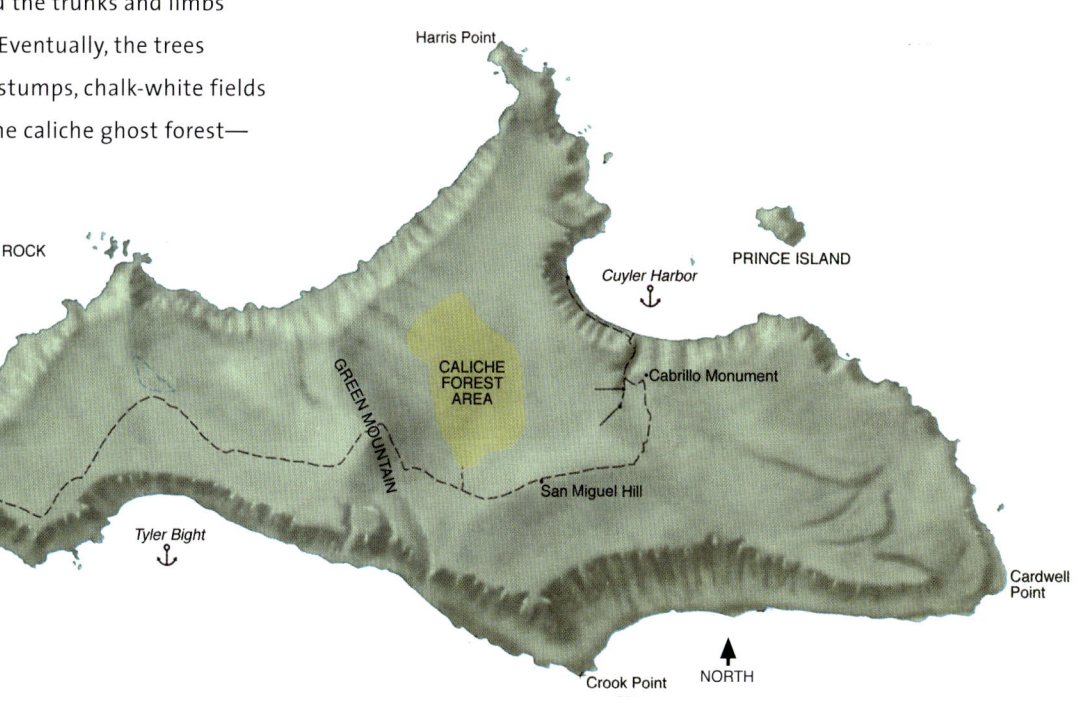

SAN MIGUEL ISLAND 99

A sudden fog-drift muffles the ocean.
A throbbing of engines moved in it.
At length, a stone's throw out, between the rocks and the vapor.
One by one moved shadows
Out of the mystery, shadows, fishing-boats, trailing each other
Following the cliff for guidance.
Holding a difficult path between the peril of the sea-fog
And the foam on the shore granite.

          Robinson Jeffers
          Boats in a Fog (1987)

Cuyler Harbor.

Visitors land by skiff at Cuyler Harbor.

Prince Island, a forty-acre island located within Cuyler Harbor, has the densest seabird colony in Southern California, with eleven different breeding species.

Opposite page: Summer-blooming red buckwheat follows spring displays of giant coreopsis in Nidever Canyon.

Above: Brightened by red Indian paintbrush, Nidever Canyon is the only access to the island from Cuyler Harbor.

Flowers were plentiful that spring because of the winter's heavy rains. The dunes were covered with mats of sand flowers, which are red and have tiny eyes that are sometimes pink and sometimes white. Yuccas grew tall among the rocks of the ravine. Their heads were clustered with curly globes no larger than pebbles and the color of the sun when it rises. Lupines grew where the springs ran. From the sunny cliffs, in crevices where no one would think anything could grow, sprang the little red and yellow fountains of the comul bush.

    Scott O'Dell
    Island of the Blue Dolphins (1960)

Opposite page: A magnificent floral display along Harris Point Trail.
Above: California poppy.

Caliche forest.

The sculpting power of wind has created spectacular examples of caliche.

An uncanny phenomena of San Miguel Island is the sound of passing ships in the Santa Barbara Channel. These sounds are felt more than heard. Yet, the ships are so far away that they cannot be seen. The vibrations just seem to come up from the ground. On windy nights, the chanting voices of Indian women may be heard somewhere off to the west of the ranch house. The howling wind blowing through the grass, barrancas, and the numerous sea shells left behind by the Indians creates this illusion.

ELIZABETH SHERMAN LESTER
The Legendary King of San Miguel: Island Life in the Santa Barbara Channel (1974)

Opposite page: Intricately carved caliche in Cuyler Harbor.

Left: Midden sites, like this one near Cuyler Harbor, reveal that San Miguel Island has been occupied as long as 11,600 years.

Cardwell Point.

Above and opposite page: Northern elephant seals.

114 CHANNEL ISLANDS

Low-lying clouds and fog often obscure the upper elevations of the trail to Point Bennett.

Left: San Luis Obispo locoweed.

Right: San Miguel Island locoweed.

Left: Immense pinniped and sea bird populations use San Miguel Island and its offshore rocks such as Castle Rock, for breeding, nesting, and resting — testament to the productive food-web within these offshore waters.

Above: San Miguel Island fox.

Above: One of the world's finest displays of pinnipeds can be seen at Point Bennett.

Opposite page: Unusual rock formation near Point Bennett.

North Peak.

Santa Barbara Island
CROSSROADS OF THE ISLANDS

Out here, thirty-eight miles from the mainland, the wind really blows. Santa Barbara Island, smallest of the five islands that make up Channel Islands National Park, measures only one square mile in size. That's not much, a mere speck in the void, especially in this watery immensity. The wind sweeps the island's bleak surface with a steady hand. Visitors getting off the boat at Landing Cove after the four-hour voyage from the mainland tend to walk like tipsy sailors, rolling on wobbly feet.

Once ashore, they are bombarded by animal sounds—gulls yelping, sea lions barking—which resound with stereophonic intensity from every corner of the island. Santa Barbara Island may be tiny in size, but its location on the fringe of the Pacific Ocean makes it a magnet for wildlife. The steep, cliff-like shores are lapped by a rich intertidal zone that supports a staggering array of maritime life. Kelp beds girdle the island, nurturing a wealth of aquatic species. The place is a mecca for divers.

From a mainland vantage point on a clear day, Santa Barbara Island dots the horizon like a tiny bubble. Now you see it, now you don't. From the perspective of the diminutive island, the mountains on the mainland float against the horizon like a greasy smudge. It's like standing on an elevated platform in the middle of an empty ocean and thinking you are the only person left alive on the earth.

Western gulls drift overhead, dipping with the wind, ragging and scolding. Black oystercatchers sail around the rocky edges, piercing the air with their sharp, whistly cries. On all sides sheer cliffs rise to a ridge-like marine terrace whose highest point is Signal Peak (635 feet). Critical fuel and water shortages prevented the Gabrielino people of the southern Channel Islands from establishing a permanent settlement out here; instead, paddling in their woodplank boats, they used it as a resting place during their lengthy, inter-island voyages.

Silver lotus.

European explorer Sebastian Vizcaino gave the island its name after putting ashore on Saint Barbara's Day, December 4, 1602. Who knows how many people have landed in the 400 years since to climb to the top of Signal Peak and stare out at the open sea? Aleut otter hunters, Kanaka mariners, clam and mollusk gatherers, sea lion hunters, Chinese lobster trappers. In the 1890s, H. Bayfield Webster, fresh from an exhausting effort to raise sheep on Anacapa Island, built a cabin on Santa Barbara Island at the point that now bears his name. The island's most noteworthy residents were the Alvin Hyder family, originally from San Pedro, who settled on the premises between 1914 and 1922, growing hay and herding sheep. The sheep exacted a savage toll on the island's vegetation, especially the coreopsis, a type of sunflower that blooms with dazzling radiance in the spring. The introduction of Belgian hares in 1916 compounded the problem; fields where earlier the fleshy trunks of the coreopsis had stood taller than a man were devastated by voracious rabbits.

Additional degradation occurred during World War II when the U.S. Navy established an early warning radar outpost on the island. In the 1940s, New Zealand red rabbits were brought over from the mainland and turned loose, which further decimated the coreopsis as well as the white morning glory. The National Park Service eliminated the rabbits in the 1980s. Since then, the landscape has been on the mend; nesting birds, night lizards, the island deer mouse, six species of land mollusks have all made dramatic recoveries.

Today, Santa Barbara Island provides a nourishing habitat for birds. Nearly seventy species have been observed, including three species of cormorants, Cassin's auklets, and Xantus' murrelets. Despite its modest size, the island is the second most important of the Channel Islands for nesting seabirds.

Sadly, the endemic Santa Barbara song sparrow is thought to be extinct; the last field sighting was in August 1967. On the plus side, western gulls and the endangered California brown pelican have established thriving rookeries. The population of Xantus' murrelets, numbering in the thousands, is believed to be the largest breeding colony of that species in the world. The murrelets burrow into the steep hillsides and cliffs; within forty-eight hours after hatching, the chicks plunge into the ocean, where they spend the rest of their lives before returning to the island to reproduce.

Sutil Island.

Today, visitors to Santa Barbara Island disembark at Landing Cove and hike up 160 steps to the top of the marine terrace. Approximately 5.5 miles of trails make the island's attractions easily accessible. From the cliff overlooking Elephant Seal Cove, visitors can observe the birth of sea lion pups in early summer; in the winter months, elephant seals breed and give birth at the same location. At Webster Point the trail leads past a western gull rookery, where chicks hatch in late May and early June.

Crystalline iceplant literally grows everywhere on the island. An introduced plant native to South Africa, it thrives in maritime areas with disturbed soils; its wet, fleshy leaves contain a high concentration of salt, which prevents other plant seeds from germinating.

Santa Barbara Island enjoys a more temperate climate than that of the four northern Channel Islands; daytime temperatures range from 50 to 80 degrees. On a clear day, every member of the Channel Islands chain can be seen from Santa Barbara Island, with the exception of San Miguel Island, which is concealed from view by its larger neighbor, Santa Rosa Island.

Above: A colorful display of giant coreopsis on the slopes of Signal Peak.

Opposite page: Blue dicks at the base of Signal Peak. In the distance is Sutil Island.

Opposite page: In the late spring and early summer, California sea lions aggressively protect their newborn pups from the much larger Northern elephant seals.

Above: A California sea lion and her pup basking in the sun at Elephant Seal Cove.

Opposite page: Low tides reveal an intertidal zone rich in marine life.

Above: Snorkeling in Landing Cove.

North Peak.

Top: Santa Barbara Island live-forever.

Bottom: Santa Barbara Island cream cups.
Both are endemic to Santa Barbara Island.

Above: Hikers near Webster Point.

Opposite page: One of the largest western gull rookeries in the Channel Islands is located at Webster Point. Western gulls usually lay two or three eggs per nest.

SANTA BARBARA ISLAND 135

Above: An estimated 1,200 pairs of California brown pelicans nest on Santa Barbara Island.

Opposite page: Steep, rugged cliffs such as these below Signal Peak surround much of the island.

Evening light falls across Webster Point, the westernmost tip of Santa Barbara Island.

A spectacular display of giant coreopsis dominates this view of Arch Point from Canyon View Nature Trail.

Channel Islands National Marine Sanctuary

UNDERSEA GARDEN

It's magical a few feet down in the chilly waters off the coast of tiny Santa Barbara Island, magical and a bit unsettling. Sunlight striking the surface refracts into gauzy beams that filter down through the swaying coils of kelp boughs in ghostly flashes of whitish light. Bright-colored Garibaldi, California's "marine fish", slip through a tangle of slick, swaying leaves. Curious divers find themselves the target of mirthful play by juvenile sea lions, who sneak up behind and tug the tips of their rubber fins, then speed off in a rash of bubbles.

Kelp forest. [Photo © Dan Richards/Channel Islands National Park]

The Channel Islands National Marine Sanctuary is located off the coast of Santa Barbara and Ventura counties in Southern California. The sanctuary, a special marine protected area administered by the National Oceanic and Atmospheric Administration (NOAA), includes 1,128 square nautical miles ranging from mean high tide to six nautical miles offshore of Santa Barbara, Anacapa, Santa Cruz, Santa Rosa, and San Miguel islands.

The purpose of the sanctuary is to protect the life-forms that dwell there while providing for compatible human usages such as shipping, tourism, commercial and recreational fishing. The sanctuary employs a comprehensive eco-management plan to promote long-term conservation of sanctuary waters, including wildlife, habitats, shipwrecks, and maritime heritage artifacts.

At Point Conception the California coastline swings sharply to the east. South of the point, the cold, temperate waters of the prevailing California Current flow south to converge with the warmer northbound waters of the Southern California Countercurrent to create a slow, steady, pinwheel effect that stirs up nutrients (plankton) from the bottom in a process known as upwelling.

Channel Islands National Park is more than a quintet of geologically interrelated landscapes that rise out of the sea a short distance off the coast of Southern California. The sea that surrounds them contains a mystery and immensity of its own. Each island is swathed and buffered by complex intertidal zones marked by major fluctuations in moisture, temperature, and sunlight. Here, in the dramatic interface between ocean and land, a variety of creatures proliferates.

To the gravitational pull of the sun and the moon, the twice-daily tides in the Santa Barbara Channel creep up the boundary reefs and beaches of the rims of the five islands before falling away to expose the tide pools to the regenerative light of the sun. The influx of chilly seawater helps sow nutrients throughout the eroded holes and pockets that gouge the rims. The tidal range on the five islands within the sanctuary is approximately seven feet. Within that seven-foot differential, a host of creatures gestate and die.

Quietly, implacably, every moment of every day, a fierce Darwinian struggle takes place between these contending life-forms. Tide pools offer a look at the marine world in miniature, a place where countless creatures play out the dictates of their complex biological urges in a bewildering variety of ways. Filter feeders such as mussels and clams take in and expel water, retaining the nutrients. Herbivores such as the giant keyhole limpet feed on algae by scraping the rocks with their coarse, tongue-like radula. Sea stars laze around the rocky ledges, opening the shells of basking mussels with their nimble feet and absorbing the tender flesh. The sculpin, deftly camouflaged with a mottled coloration—the most commonly found fish in the tide-pool world—picks off unsuspecting prey such as small crabs.

Below the intertidal zone dwell the deep beds of giant kelp, a type of brown alga that grows faster than any other plant on earth. Under favorable conditions—ample nutrients, a rocky substrate, between twenty and eighty feet of cool seawater—kelp can grow at the astounding rate of two feet per day.

The normal life span of a single frond of giant kelp is six months; at that rate, as part of its natural cycle, the forest may completely regenerate itself twice a year. Anchored to rocks by a mass of tangled strands, the sturdy yet flexible fronds rise to the surface, where, buoyed by gas-filled floats that grow at the base of the wrinkled leaves, they intertwine to form a thick, shadowy canopy. The dangling strands provide a dense, multilayered home for nearly a thousand different plant and animal species, ranging from tiny bryozoans to gigantic gray whales—an ocean ecosystem comparable in many respects to a tropical rainforest.

Aerial view of islands and sanctuary.

Over 125 types of fish live in the kelp forest. The sleek, tangled vines serve as a temporary stop for piscines such as the keop bass, bat ray, and topsmelt. Sheephead lurk in the kelp beds, poised to consume their favorite food, the spiny urchin, while remaining oblivious to the sharp spines that get stuck in their gill covers.

But it's not all about little critters in the Santa Barbara Channel. Over twenty-eight species of dolphins and whales, including the titanic blue whale, the biggest mammal on earth, pass through or linger within the boundaries of the Channel Islands National Marine Sanctuary.

The Santa Barbara Channel is one of the premier places in the world to view cetaceans. The yearly migrations of gray whales from their birthing grounds in Baja California to their summer feeding grounds off the coast of Alaska draw thousands of people from all over the world. The leviathans follow a well-defined route that takes them a distance of 10,000 miles—the longest known migration by any mammal on earth. The gray whales, with their predictable itinerary and their habit of traveling close to shore, are the easiest to observe.

Few places in the world can match the Channel Islands for the number and variety of seals and sea lions found there. Seals and sea lions are pinnipeds (literally "feather footed"), adapted to both aquatic and terrestrial life; coated with thick layers of insulating fat, they remain impervious to chilly ocean water. A total of six types of pinnipeds, including California sea lions, elephant seals, and harbor seals, depend on the sanctuary for feeding and breeding.

Seabirds thrive on the welter of food they find on and around the islands. The many tidepools and kelp forests bobbing offshore offer a fabulous trove of edible stuff. More than sixty species feed in the waters of the Channel Islands National Marine Sanctuary during part of the year; eleven species are known to breed here. Of the islands that lie within the sanctuary, San Miguel Island boasts the most diverse and abundant concentration of breeding seabirds.

Top: California sheephead. [Photo © Kathy deWet-Oleson]

Bottom: Club-tipped anemone. [Photo © Steven Trainoff]

To witness 2,000 common dolphins engaged in a feeding frenzy is an experience not soon forgotten.

Poetry in motion, as a humpback whale gracefully slips below the surface of the sea.

Top left: **Spiny brittle star.** [Photo © Kathy deWet-Oleson]

Top right: **White-spotted rose anemone.** [Photo © Steven Trainoff]

Bottom left: **Spanish shawl.** [Photo © Steven Trainoff]

Bottom right: **Spiny brittle star.** [Photo © Kathy deWet-Oleson]

Opposite page: A spectacular sea fan, the California golden gorgonian dominates this colorful scene on the Anacapa Reef, near Anacapa Island.

Red gorgonian. [Photo © Kathy deWet-Oleson]

The inquisitive California Garibaldi is the official "marine fish" of the state of California.
[Photo © Channel Islands National Marine Sanctuary]

The bat ray often feeds on clams and other organisms found on the ocean floor. [Photo © Kathy deWet-Oleson]

A market squid with a cluster of egg casings, each casing containing as many as 200 fertilized eggs. [Photo © Kathy deWet-Oleson]

Opposite page: The odd-shaped mola mola, sometimes called the ocean sunfish, is the heaviest bony fish in the world, with an average weight of 2,000 pounds. [Photo © Steven Trainoff]

Above: Swordtail squid [Photo © Kathy deWet-Oleson]

Pacific barracuda. [Photo © Stuart Halewood]

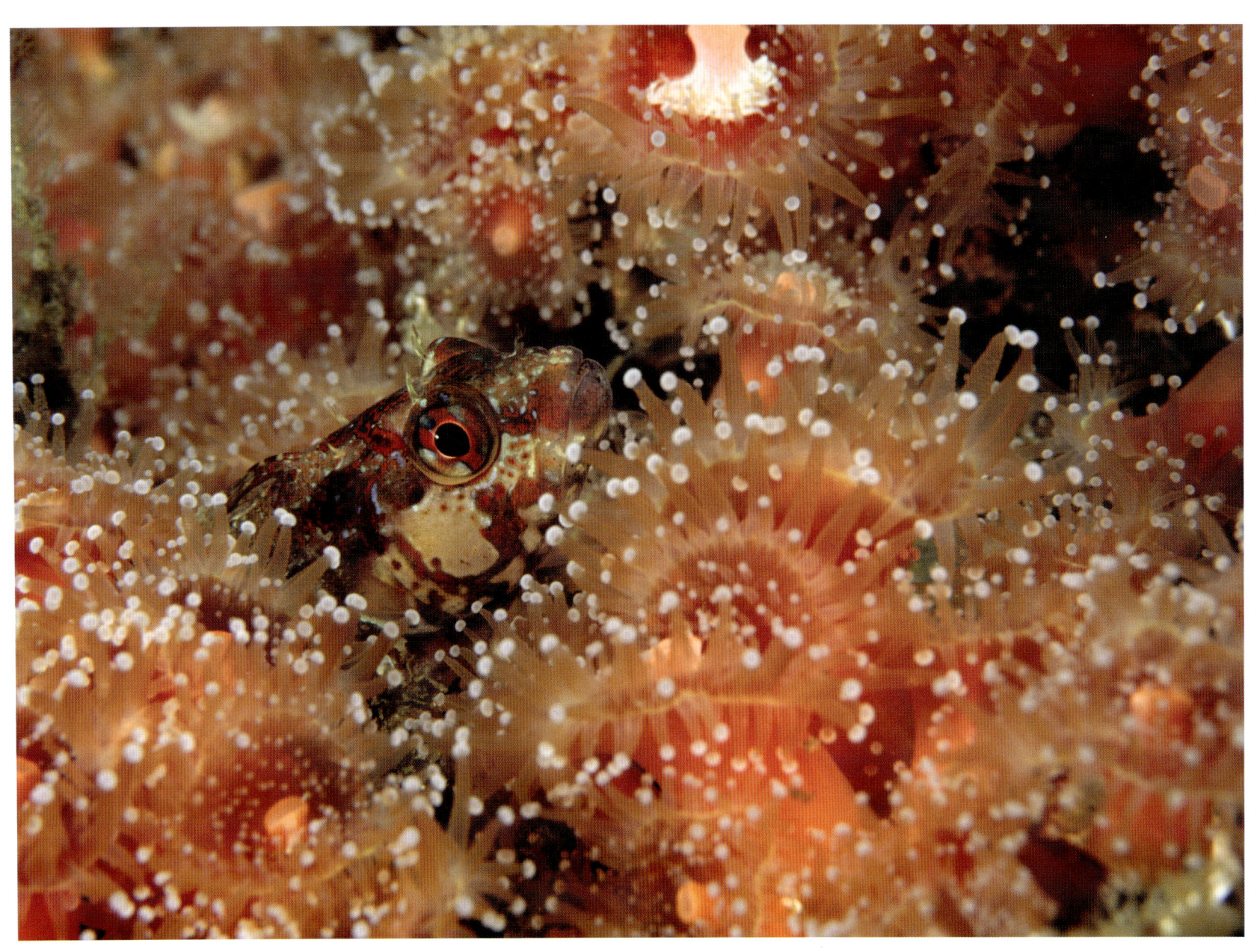

Camouflage is necessary for survival in the ocean. Here an island kelpfish hides among club-tipped anemone.

[Photo © Kathy deWet-Oleson]

The cabezon is a bottom-dwelling sculpin, waiting for prey as it takes advantage of its mottled coloration. [Photo © Steven Trainoff]

Appendix

This appendix is a scientific listing of the plants and animals shown or referred to in this book. It is not intended as a complete listing of all the plants and animals that can be found on or around the Channel Islands.

TERRESTRIAL PLANTS
Bishop Pine *(Pinus muricata)*
Blue Dick *(Dichelostemma capitatum)*
Blue-eyed Grass *(Sisyrinchium bellum)*
Bush Monkey Flower *(Mimulus longiflorus)*
California Poppy *(Eschscholzia californica)*
Candleholder Dudleya *(Dudleya candelabrum)*
Checker Bloom *(Sidalcea malviflora)*
Coastal Cholla *(Opuntia prolifera)*
Coastal Sagebrush *(Artemisia californica)*
Common Monkey Flower *(Mimulus guttatus)*
Giant Coreopsis *(Coreopsis gigantea)*
Golden Yarrow *(Eriophyllum confertiflorum)*
Goldfields *(Lathenia californica)*
Greene's Live-forever *(Dudleya greenei)*
Indian Paintbrush *(Castilleja affinis)*
Island Big-pod Ceanothus *(Ceanothus megacarpus ssp. insularis)*
Island Bush Poppy *(Dendromecon harfordii)* **1**
Island Cherry *(Prunus ilicifolia subsp. Lyonii)*
Island Cliff-aster *(Malacothrix saxatilis var. implicata)*
Island Manzanita *(Arctostaphylos tomentosa subsp. insulicola)*
Island Monkey Flower *(Mimulus flemingii)*
Island Morning Glory *(Calystegia macrostegia subsp. macrostegia)*
Island Oak *(Quercus tomentella)*
Island Torrey Pine *(Pinus torreyana subsp. insularis)* **2**
McMinn's Manzanita *(Arctostaphylos viridissima)* **1**
Mediterranean Canary Grass *(Phalaris minor)*
Munchkin Dudleya *(Dudleya gnoma)* **2**
Purple Owl's Clover *(Castilleja exserta)*
Rancheria Clover *(Trifolium albopurpureum)*
Red Buckwheat *(Eriogonum grande var. rubescens)*
Rock Daisy *(Perityle emoryi)*
San Luis Obispo Locoweed *(Astragalus curtipes)*
San Miguel Island Locoweed *(Astragalus miguelenis)*
Santa Barbara Island Cream Cups *(Platystemon californicus var. ciliatus)* **3**
Santa Barbara Island Live-forever *(Dudleya traskiae)* **3 E**
Santa Cruz Island Gooseberry *(Ribes thacherianum)* **1**
Santa Cruz Island Ironwood *(Lyonothamnus floribundus subsp. aspleniifolius)*
Santa Cruz Island Lace Pod *(Thysanocarpus conchuliferus)* **1 E**
Santa Cruz Island Mallow *(Malacothamnus fasiculatus ssp. nesioticus)* **1 E**
Santa Cruz Island Manzanita *(Arctostaphylos insularis)* **1**
Santa Cruz Island Monkey Flower *(Mimulus brandegeei)* **1**
Santa Cruz Island Silver Lotus *(Lotus argophyllus var. niveus)* **1**
Sea Rocket *(Cakile maritima)*
Seaside Daisy *(Erigeron glaucus)*
Silver Lotus *(Lotus argophyllus var. ornithopus)*
Snow Berry *(Symphoricarpos mollis)*
Subcordate Manzanita *(Arctostaphylos tomentosa subsp. subcordata)*
Succulent Lupine *(Lupinus succulentus)*
Trask's Locoweed *(Astragalus traskiae)*
Yarrow *(Achillea millefolium)*

MARINE PLANTS
Agar Weed *(Gelidium)*
Brown Algae *(Halidrys dioica)*
California Golden Gorgonian *(Muricea californica)*
Coralline Algae *(Bossiella)* or *(Calliarthron)*
Giant Bladder Kelp *(Bacrocystis pyrifera)*
Red Gorgonian *(Lophogorgia chilensis)*

BIRDS
Black Oystercatcher *(Haematopus bachmani)*
Brandt's Cormorant *(Phalacrocorax penicillatus)*
California Brown Pelican *(Pelecanus occidentalis)* **E**
Cassin's Auklet *(Ptychoramphus aleuticus)*
European Starling *(Sturnus vulgaris)*
Long-billed Curlew *(Numenius americanus)*
Pigeon Guillemot *(Cepphus columba)*
Sanderling *(Calidris alba)*
Santa Barbara Song Sparrow *(Melospiza melodia graminea)* (extinct)
Santa Cruz Island Jay *(Aphelocoma coerulescens insularis)* **1**
Western Gull *(Larus occidentalis)*
Western Snowy Plover *(Charadrius alexandrinus nivosus)* **T**
Whimbrel *(Numenius phaeopus)*
Xantus Murrelet *(Synthliboramphus hypolecus)*

TERRESTRIAL ANIMALS
Deer Mouse *(Peromyscus maniculatus)*
Island Night Lizard *(Xantusia riversiana)* **T**
San Miguel Island Fox *(Urocyon littoralis littoralis)* **4 E**
Santa Cruz Island Fox *(Urocyon littoralis santacruzae)* **1 E**
Santa Rosa Island Fox *(Urocyon littoralis santarosae)* **2 E**
Spotted Skunk *(Spilogale gracilis amphiala)*
Western Harvest Mouse *(Reithrodontomys megalotis)*

MARINE ANIMALS
Bat Ray *(Myliobatis californica)*
Blue Whale *(Balaenoptera musculus)* **E**
Cabezon *(Scorpaenichthys marmoratus)*
California Garibaldi *(Hypsypops rubicundus)*
California Gray Whale *(Eschrichtius robustus)*
California Sea Lion *(Zalophus californianus)*
California Sheephead *(Semicossyphus pulcher)*
Club-Tipped Anemone *(Corynactis californica)*
Common Dolphin *(Delphinus capensis)* (Long beaked)
Common Dolphin *(Delphinus delphis)* (Short beaked)
Giant Keyhole Limpet *(Megathura crenulata)*
Green Sea Anemone *(Anthpleura elegantissima)*
Guadalupe Fur Seal *(Arctocephalus townsendi)* **T**
Harbor Seal *(Phoca vitulina)*
Humpback Whale *(Megaptera novaeangliae)* **T**
Island Kelpfish *(Alloclinus holderi)*
Knobby Star *(Pisaster giganteus)*
Market Squid *(Loligo opalescens)* {on egg cases}
Northern Elephant Seal *(Mirounga angustirostris)*
Northern Fur Seal *(Callorhinus ursinus)*
Ocean Sunfish or Mola Mola *(Mola mola)*
Ochre Starfish *(Pisaster ochraceus)*
Pacific Barracuda *(Sphyraena argentea)*
Sea Jelly *(Polyorchis penicillatus)*
Spanish Shawl *(flabellina iodinea)*
Spiny Brittle Star *(Ophiothrix spiculata)*
Stellar Sea Lion *(Eumetopias jubatus)* **T**
Swordtail Squid *(Chiroteuthis calyx)*
White-Spotted Rose Anemone *(Urticina lofotensis)*

LEGEND
E Endangered
T Threatened
1 Endemic to Santa Cruz Island
2 Endemic to Santa Rosa Island
3 Endemic to Santa Barbara Island
4 Endemic to San Miguel Island

Bibliography

Agenbroad, Larry D. *Pygmy (Dwarf) Mammoths of the Channel Islands of California.* Mammoth Site of Hot Springs, SD, Inc., 1998.

Allen, Kerry Blankenship, editor. *Island of the Cowboys: Santa Rosa Island.* Santa Barbara: Santa Cruz Island Foundation, 1996.

Angel, Myron. *The Painted Rock: A Legend.* San Luis Obispo: Padre Publications, 1979.

Batman, Richard. *The Outer Coast.* New York: Harcourt Brace Jovanovich, 1985.

Bean, Lowell John, and Thomas C. Blackburn, editors. *Native Californians: A Theoretical Retrospective.* Socorro, NM: Ballena Press, 1976.

Beasley, Conger, Jr. *Eyes Open in the Dark: Eight Essays.* Kansas City: BkMk Press, 1996.

Blackburn, Thomas C., editor. *December's Child: A Book of Chumash Oral Narratives.* Berkeley: University of California Press, 1980.

California's Chumash Indians. Santa Barbara: Santa Barbara Museum of Natural History, 1986.

Carson, Rachel. *The Sea Around Us.* New York: New American Library, 1954.

Daily, Marla. *California's Channel Islands: 1001 Questions Answered.* Santa Barbara: McNally & Loftin Publishers, 1987.

Daily, Marla, editor. *Santa Barbara Island.* Santa Barbara: Santa Cruz Island Foundation, 1993.

Daily, Marla, editor. *Santa Cruz Island Anthology.* Santa Barbara: Santa Cruz Island Foundation, 1989.

Daily, Marla, editor. *A Step Back in Time: Unpublished Channel Islands Diaries.* Santa Barbara: Santa Cruz Island Foundation, 1990.

Dana, Richard Henry. *Two Years before the Mast.* New York: Modern Library, 1936.

Defoe, Daniel. *Robinson Crusoe.* New York: Random House, 1948.

Dogen. *Moon in a Dewdrop: Writings of Zen Master Dogen.* New York: North Point Press, 1985.

Dowty, Karen Jones. *The California Channel Islands.* Ventura: A Seaquit Book, 1987.

Durrell, Lawrence. *Prospero's Cell.* New York: E. P. Dutton & Company, 1960.

Durrell, Lawrence. *Reflections on a Marine Venus.* New York: E. P. Dutton and Company, 1960.

Eaton, Margaret Holden. *Diary of a Sea Captain's Wife: Tales of Santa Cruz Island.* Santa Barbara: McNally & Loftin, 1980.

Ehrlich, Gretel. *Cowboy Island: Farewell to a Ranching Legacy.* Santa Barbara: Santa Cruz Island Foundation, 2000.

Ellison, William Henry, editor. *The Life and Adventures of George Nidever [1802–1883].* Santa Barbara: McNally & Loftin, 1984.

Exupery, Antoine de Saint. *Wind, Sand and Stars.* New York: Reynal & Hitchcock, 1939.

Gherini, John. *Santa Cruz Island: A History of Conflict and Diversity.* Spokane: The Arthur H. Clark Company, 1997.

Gibson, Robert O. *The Chumash.* New York: Chelsea House, 1991.

Grant, Campbell. *The Rock Paintings of the Chumash.* Berkeley: University of California Press, 1965.

Hauf, Tim. *Channel Islands National Park: A Photographic Interpretation.* Somis: Tim Hauf Photography, 1996.

Hawley, Walter A. *The Early Days of Santa Barbara, California: From the First Discoveries by Europeans to December, 1846.* Santa Barbara: Santa Barbara Heritage, 1987.

Hoffmann, Eleanor. *The Charmstone.* Santa Barbara: McNally and Loftin, 1981.

Howe, Sheri. *Mirounga: A Guide to Elephant Seals.* Davenport, CA: Frank S. Balthis, 1986.

Hudson, Travis. *Guide to Painted Cave.* Santa Barbara: Santa Barbara Museum of Natural History, 1982.

Jeffers, Robinson. *Rock and Hawk: A Selection of Shorter Poems,* edited by Robert Hass. New York: Random House, 1987.

Lamb, Susan. *Channel Islands National Park.* Tucson: Western National Parks Association, 2000.

Lester, Elizabeth Sherman. *The Legendary King of San Miguel: Island Life in the Santa Barbara Channel.* Santa Barbara: McNally & Loftin, 1974.

McElrath, Clifford. *On Santa Cruz Island: The Ranching Recollections of Clifford McElrath.* Santa Barbara: Santa Barbara Historical Society, 1993.

Melville, Herman. *Complete Short Stories, "The Encantadas."* New York: Random House, 1952.

Miller, Bruce W. *Chumash: A Picture of Their World.* Los Osos: Sand River Press, 1988.

Miller, Bruce W. *The Gabrielino.* Los Osos: Sand River Press, 1991.

Nechodom, Kerry. *The Rainbow Bridge: A Chumash Legend,* illustrated by Tom Nechodom. Los Osos: Sand River Press, 1992.

O'Dell, Scott. *Island of the Blue Dolphins.* New York: Dell Publishing Co., 1960.

Sanger, Kay. *When the Animals Were People: Stories Told by the Chumash Indians of California.* Banning: Malki Museum Press, 1983.

Shakespeare, William. *The Tempest,* edited by Frank Kermode. Cambridge: Harvard University Press, 1958.

Williams, Oscar, editor. *The Mentor Book of Major British Poets.* New York: New American Library, 1963.

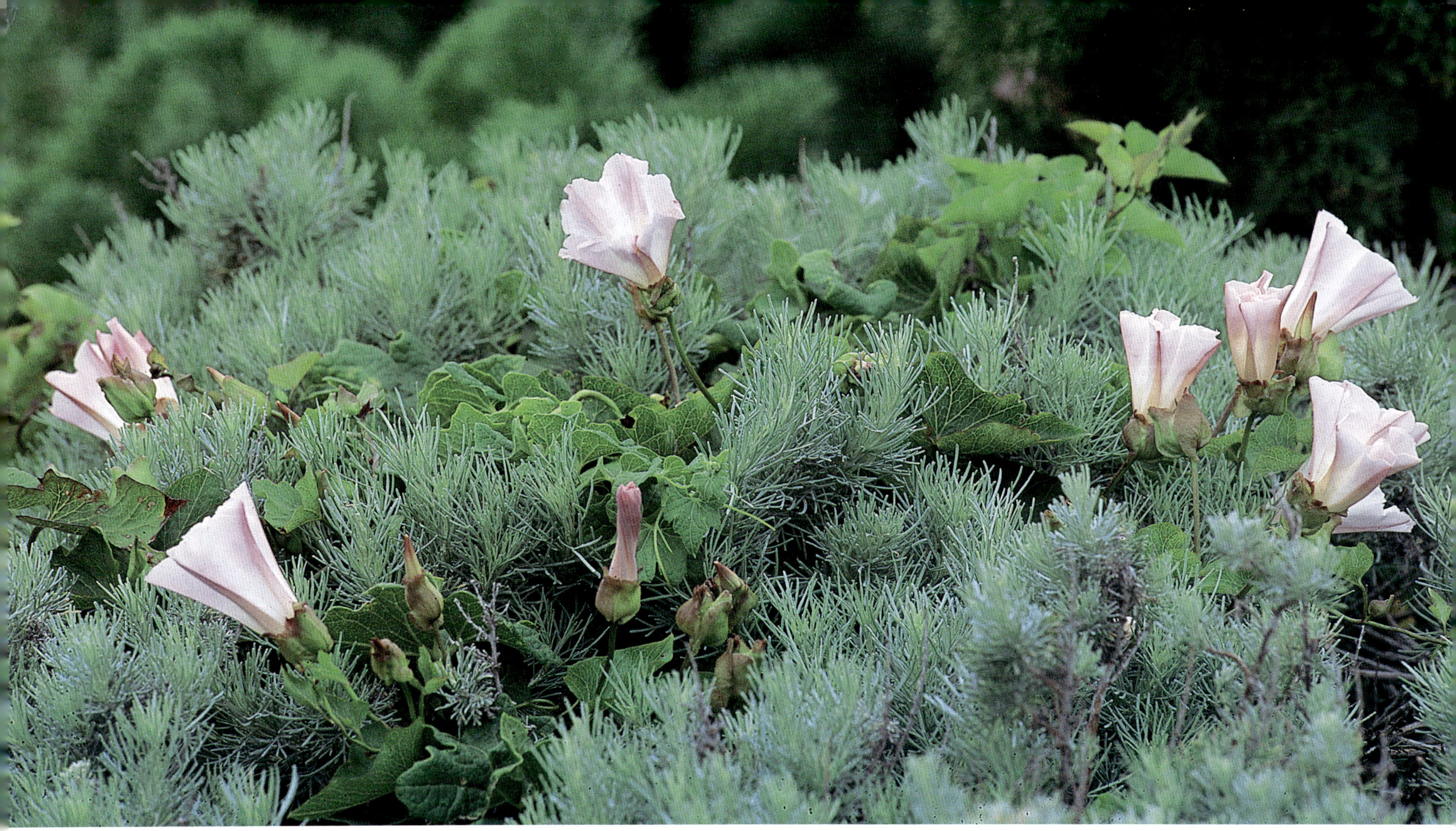

Sponsors

National Marine Sanctuaries™
Channel Islands

Island Packers
Since 1968

Ventura
Visitors & Convention Bureau

Ventura County Maritime Museum
at Channel Islands Harbor

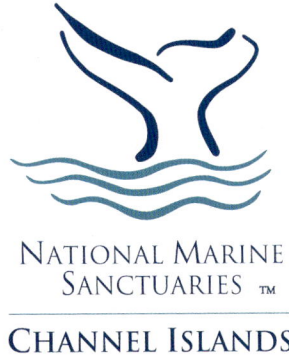

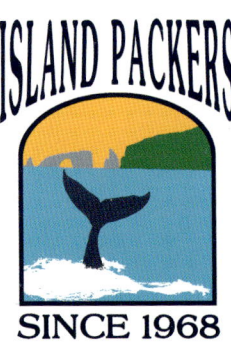

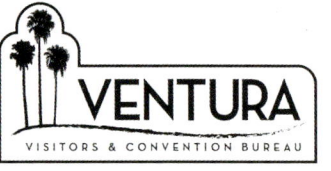

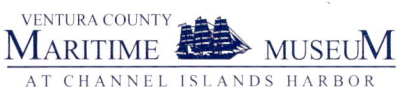